Volker Bender

The Koblenz Cable Car

A brief guide for technical and
non-technical readers

Imprint

All rights reserved. This book or any portion thereof may not be reproduced or used in any manner whatsoever without the express written permission of the publisher except for the use of brief quotations in abook review.

Bibliografische Information der Deutschen Nationalbibliothek:
Die Deutsche Nationalbibliothek verzeichnet diese Publikation in der Deutschen Nationalbibliografie; detaillierte bibliografische Daten sind im Internet über http://dnb.dnb.de abrufbar.

© 2017 Volker Bender
Photos:
Page 9,10 © by Holger Weinandt License: CC-BY-SA 3.0 via http://commons.wikimedia.org
Page U1,8,12,13,14,15,17,18,23,25,31,34 © by Doppelmayr GmbH, A-Wolfurt

Manufactured and published by: BoD – Books on Demand, Norderstedt
ISBN: 978-3-7431-6167-2

Historical Background

Perhaps the 1908 inhabitants of Koblenz envied the people of the South Tirol, since it was there that, on 29th June, they established the first cable car, to bring passengers from Bozen on the local mountain to Kohlern. Hotelier Josef Staffler's daring scheme to transport his guests out of the hot valley into the cool summer air in comfort caused a minor international sensation. The news spread quickly and soon there were reports of innovations in other regions: in 1912 another cable car began to operate in the South Tirol, followed, in 1924, by the first German narrow gauge locomotive in Oberwiesenthal.

There was much discussion of how the Rhinelanders might copy their neighbours and float up to the Ehrenbreitstein Fortress, instead of climbing up laboriously. But, in the end, the idea was rejected. The dream, however, was never quite forgotten, even though the country was to experience two world wars before the subject came to public attention again.

By that time, the reconstruction period had begun and tourism and winter sports were experiencing an unprecedented boom. In October 1950, the "Camp for Displaced Foreign Nationals" in the grounds of the fortress was closed and a dispute erupted between the city and the state over the future use of the site. The city of Koblenz proposed the construction of new housing in the fortress, to ease the considerable housing shortage, while the state favoured partial use of the facilities for tourism and, as the new owners, they had the last word.

Once more, people began to express the wish to transport locals and visitors to the city's most beautiful viewpoint in comfort and ease – much to the indignation of the Historical Preservation Society which called it a "blight on the Rhineland countryside".

In 2004, when the city of Koblenz was selected to organise a federal garden show ("Bundesgartenschau" or "Buga"), the idea of a cable car across the Rhine was reborn and – by comparison with the previous decades – everything now happened very quickly. First, expert assessments showed that the project was technically and financially viable. The city, Buga GmbH and UNESCO just had to pull together, since UNESCO had just awarded the Upper Middle Rhine Valley World Heritage Site status, in 2002.

UNESCO weren't prepared to countenance the permanent installation of a cable car, but they expressed their willingness to accept a temporary solution,. which would have to be dismantled two years after the end of the Buga. It was a compromise people could live with. The first task was to find the best location for the lower station. The planners initially considered eight alternatives, but, by the end, only two practicable options remained: one led up to the fortress from the campsite in the Lützel neighbourhood and the other from the current location on the bank of the Rhine. Lützel had the disadvantage of requiring a Mosel crossing. Visitors would have had to be guided over a pedestrian bridge, leading from the Deutsches Eck to the lower station. A smaller cable car – a "feeder" to bring passengers from the Deutsches Eck to the opposite bank of the Mosel – would have meant huge additional expense.

A lower station on the bank of the Rhine had the disadvantage of being in the immediate vicinity of the St Castor basilica. In the end, however, despite all reservations, the Buga representatives decided to favour this "short" route from the bank of the Rhine to the fortress and authorise the construction of a cable car.

At the end of 2008, the Doppelmayr Group from Wolfurt, Austria, were awarded the commission to undertake the project and run it as a concession for three years. The decisive factor was that the Austrians' offer fulfilled UNESCO requirements, making do with only two supports, which allowed them to avoid excessive damage to the historic image of the fortifications and hillside.

Construction

The work began in April 2009 when the first trees were felled. One month later, the lower station's 16-metre deep foundations had already been laid. The technicians used the hardest concrete commercially available to resist the immense tensile force of the cables. The lower station's machinery was simultaneously constructed in Wolfurt and individual parts were put together on a trial basis.

The shell was completed by late summer, shortly after which the Austrians arrived with seven articulated lorries. 120 tonnes of material were unloaded in Koblenz on the banks of the Rhine and individual segments of machinery were pre-sorted. The pieces were gradually put together and the cable car's centrepiece, its powerful red pulleys, were towed into position. Later, they would support the traction cable which would move the cars.

At the same time, they were working on the upper station. Its support, a 25-metre tall steel girder, weighed 90 tonnes. The cables would later run over the saddle pulleys, attached to the top.

Specialists from Switzerland were flown in to connect the upper and lower stations. Over the following months, they applied themselves to "hoisting the cable", as the task of raising and tightening the cable of a cable car is called in the professional lingo of that trade. Despite careful planning, it was no easy task in Koblenz, in the tight space over a federal waterway and next to a busy railway line.

In January 2010, they were finally ready: following a meticulously prepared action plan, federal highway 42 was blocked off, shipping on the Rhine was halted and rail services suspended.

A helicopter rose up over the upper station. A 20-metre long catchment line was attached to its rear end and dangled high above the cable car's support. Installation technicians had been patiently enduring sub-zero temperatures for some time, waiting to guide the helicopter by radio and provide instructions. After several attempts, the men managed to knot the end of a nylon cable through the loop. The helicopter glided down the slope and delivered its cargo to the east bank of the Rhine.

The first critical hurdle had been cleared. Four days later, two lead cables were attached to the nylon cable and transported to the opposite bank of the river on a floating pontoon. During the crossing, the technicians watched eagle eyed to ensure the tension was kept constant. A torn cable would have had catastrophic consequences and could have literally struck people close by dead, while a cable which sagged too low could get wet and be rendered unusable. The enterprise succeeded on the first attempt. Once the upper

and lower stations had been connected, the cables were tightened across the Rhine. They were gradually replaced by stronger and stronger ropes, until finally the first of the 50-tonne pulley cables were stretched across the Rhine. From a dizzying height, two installation technicians screwed an auxiliary clamp onto the cable in order to tighten it, haul it into the station and anchor it there. In March 2010, both lines were pulled taut and the cable sliders – the numbered triangles which you can see arranged along the cable – were attached.

The pulley cable, whose loose ends still needed to be secured, was now fed over the cable slider, to form an unbroken ring. To achieve this, the Swiss technicians unbraided the end pieces to a length of 70 m, in order to intertwine the two ends again. This technique, known in the cable car branch as "splicing," has been mastered by only a few experts worldwide. Afterwards, the joint – the "splice" – is scarcely perceptible to the untrained eye.

In Koblenz, the "splicing" also worked right away and the two ends of the pulley cable were securely joined. Now the cable needed to complete a "circuit." The technicians tightened it and switched on the motors. The powerful pulleys slowly began to turn until the pulley cable was describing a precise circuit through the two stations in an unending loop. The first trip was reserved for the technicians. Standing on the roof of the car, with one installer even perched up on the moving cable, they descended into the valley on 29th April, to loud applause from the citizens of Koblenz. The journey had taken place without any major problems. They could now begin making the final adjustments.

Meanwhile, the upper and lower stations were continuing to take shape. The Werner Sobek group from Stuttgart had developed a sheath to protect them from the weather. The cloth mesh, only a millimetre thick, concealed the concrete pedestals with their massive machinery. Illuminated by night, they made the stations look like alien structures, seemingly hovering above the ground.

By May 2010, all the cars had been mounted onto the pulley cable. A brief three-month season began in July. In the first month, the passengers already numbered 50,000 and, by the end, the total number was almost 180,000. Six months later, on the 15th April, 2001, regular service began, with the opening of the Federal Garden Show.

In total, nearly 100 cable car and wire cable experts spent more than a year constructing the system which made possible the first German cable car in an urban area.

Technology and Operation

General

The Koblenz cable car consists of an elliptical track made up of three cables and is therefore also known as a three-cable or tri-cable system (3S) cable car, characterised by two supporting cables and a continuously rotating pulley cable to transport the cars. 3S cable cars are considered the most technologically advanced cable car constructions.

They are distinguished by high wind resistance and low energy use, while allowing vast numbers of passengers to be transported in both directions at once. The tri-cable technology combines the advantages of gondola with those of aerial tramway technology, permitting the development of a detachable track with a capacity of up to 35 passengers per car. However, the 3S only requires one support at each station since the significant distance between them allows for

maximum spans, enabling transportation high over rivers and city neighbourhoods. An evacuation plan, pioneered by the Koblenz cable car company, allows passengers, in the case of a system failure, to be transported to the nearest station in their cars, instead of having to be winched down. Once there, they can disembark as usual, until the entire system has gradually been "emptied."

Two machine operators at each station are responsible for the smooth running of the system. An operations manager or their deputy manager is also required to be present. The machine operators must be professionally qualified mechanics, metalworkers or electricians; the deputy manager must have at least a master craftsman's diploma in one of those professions; and the operations manager must have at least an engineering diploma. All technical assistants must be vertigo-free and have to provide a current medical certificate at regular intervals.

Safety

Statistically speaking, only one mode of transport is safer than the cable car: the passenger lift. But, unlike the lift, cable cars were developed to withstand extreme weather conditions and operate reliably in ice, snow and wind speeds of up to 100 km/h. Regular maintenance and checks of the cable car, cables and safety provisions are legally mandated. These are supervised by the regulatory authorities: in Rhineland-Pfalz, the "Agency for Mobility."

A comprehensive test of the site and its safety provisions takes place twice yearly. One of these inspections is carried out by the cable car company itself, the second by an officially recognised inspection agency. There is also mandatory daily, weekly and monthly inspection and maintenance work. In addition, a cable car system's crucial technical functions and fixtures must be checked daily, before the start of operations.

The 3S system also provides additional safety through redundancy. All functionally relevant system components, for example, pulleys, motors and emergency motors, have been duplicated, without exception, and arranged independently of each other. In the case of the steering mechanism, an error-proof, programmable logic controller ensures smooth operation of travel.

Monitoring sensors and switches signal any irregularities and, depending on their cause, may produce an immediate system halt.

The functions related to the coupling procedure for the cars at the stations are also permanently monitored. Incorrectly coupled cars are identified by sensors which bring the cable car to an immediate standstill. Cabin doors, which were not properly shut during the exit, also cause the cable car to automatically stop.

A ring circuit allows for the constant provision of electricity from two sides. In the event of a power failure, both the upper and lower stations have one available diesel engine each. This makes it possible to move the pulley cable in the event of a jammed motor, and evacuate the cars at

the stations, allowing both the track and the gondolas to be "emptied." Should the cable sheave bearings refuse to function, emergency failsafe bearings will take over their task for a limited time. This measure also ensures that the cars can be drawn into the stations.

Although it was constructed for extreme winters, the Koblenz cable car enjoys a relatively frost-free existence: as long as the Rhine does not freeze over, it gives off so much heat from below that there is no need to fear an ice build-up on the cables or car mechanisms. Before the start of operations, a daily trial run is carried out, at walking pace, in order to check the cable sliders, among other things.

The station manager has access to monitors which continually display information and technical readings. He or she can display additional details, such as wind speed, at the touch of a button. The 3S cable car is "wind stable"

at up to 22 metres per second: at 24 metres the staff receive a "wind warning" and at 26 metres a clearly audible "wind alarm." However, there is no automatic shut-down in very strong wind conditions – the station manager can decide whether the cable car can and should continue to run.

Cables

Swiss company Fatzer AG was commissioned to produce the "rails" – the Koblenz cable car's cables. The specialised firm manufactures cables from cold-drawn steel wire, a production method which results in extreme tensile strength. The Koblenz cable car incorporates four firmly anchored suspension cables with a 54 mm diameter.

At both stations, they have been wrapped around large bollards several times and their degree of tension can be corrected hydraulically if necessary. One of the suspension cables is equipped with a continuous internal cable: this integrated fibre optic cable carries analogue and digital signals between the two stations.

During the "cable hoist," the mounting of the cables, the suspension pulley is formed into a ring ("spliced"). The revolving cable has a 42 mm diameter, is flexible and is fitted with a plastic core, the so-called "soul." The traction cable is also extended using a hydraulic system, using a tension carriage to ensure the tension remains constant. It is supported by cable sliders – suspension gauges mounted on rollers – placed at regular intervals along the track. There are four of these on each "track" – preventing excessive slack over the 850 metre stretch.

Motors

The motor is activated at the upper station. A three-phase 1300 horsepower motor provides the operating power. The gear mechanism works directly on the pulley. The motor and gears are connected by a chain coupler, which can be detached if the propulsion motor is jammed, so that the traction cable can be moved using the emergency motor.

The upper and lower stations are each equipped with a 223 horsepower diesel motor, which can provide emergency power in the event of a malfunction of the electrical motor. In an emergency, the hydrostatic motor system ensures that all cars can be brought back to the stations. An inbuilt hydraulically ventilated disk brake acts as a service brake.

As soon as the cable car starts up, the brake is hydraulically released. The disk brake ensures speedy and safe braking right up to standstill in the event of a power cut or safety warning. The planners also provided duplicates of the brakes. If the service brake malfunctions, an emergency stop button is pressed or a critical speed (>10%) is reached, additional safety brakes will be activated which work directly on both sides of the pulley cable.

Cars & Driver Mechanisms

Eighteen cars with the capacity to house 35 passengers each ensure the 3S cable car's high transport capabilities. All the cars are continually in service, since the originally projected operation life of only three years did not anticipate the decommissioning ("garaging") of individual gondolas. When the cable car is not in service, nine gondolas are parked in each station, protected from wind and weather.

The drivers roll along the supporting cables. The cars are suspended from them by a rigid steel yoke. The steel yoke is positioned such that it can turn, allowing the cars to swing in both directions of travel. For the passengers, this has the fortunate effect of perceptibly cushioning the start-up and acceleration forces.

A car, the driver mechanism and 35 passengers result in a total weight of approx. 6.8 tonnes. The load is transferred to the suspension cable by 8 large rollers. They are padded by elastic, abrasion-proof plastic and are characterised by a high degree of "smooth operation."

During the journey, two mutually independent coupling grips ensure a safe, firm connection between the driver and the traction cable. This is another example of redundant construction: should one of the two grips fail, the second will allow the car to be taken to the nearest station for evacuation.

A forced guidance system permits the coupling and decoupling of the cars at the stations. During the decoupling, the driver is released from the suspension cable and rolls on along the rails of the station's stretch of track. Above the drivers, slowly rotating car tyres transfer their kinetic energy to the drivers through chequer plate.

This allows the cars to glide through the stations at a snail's pace of around 0.15 metres per second – allowing plenty of time for passengers to get on and off. Once they have cleared the boarding area, the gondolas are accelerated back up to the speed of the traction cable and automatically recoupled.

Supports

UNESCO's stipulations for the approval of a cable car at the mid Rhine World Cultural Heritage Site require the construction of a cable car with only two supports, in order to do as little damage as possible to the historic image of the fortifications, Rhine and city skyline.

The Koblenz cable car's supports are made of a round-pipe latticework and are accessible by means of ladders and work platforms. The bearer cable saddles were mounted at its "head." The traction cable rests inside, cushioned by rubber. The 850 metre span between the supports does not present a particular challenge for a cable car of the tri-cable generation.

Impressions

Careful observers will have noticed that the cable car drives on the left. This is because of local conditions, such as the positions of the boarding and disembarking zones in the Koblenz stations. During its daily operations, the cars glide from valley to mountain and back again almost silently, as if on rails.

The gondolas were specifically designed for the Buga, so even at maximum capacity, the panoramic cars offer all 35 passengers a perfect view. The cable car was intentionally fitted out as a "summer cable car." An ingenious seating design allows people to observe the happenings on the Rhine and along the banks of the river either seated, leaning in a slightly more upright position or standing. Before the introduction of 3S technology, passengers were discouraged from standing up in gondolas for fear this might cause the

cars to sway. On the tri-cable cars, vertical and horizontal handrails in the passenger section, similar to those on buses, trams and subway trains, invite standing passengers to hold on. The passenger feels as though he or she were using a form of public transport, a sensation which can reduce some passengers' fear of heights. All cars have video surveillance and are equipped with an intercom system – this also increases many passengers' feelings of safety.

The standard cars (nos. 1 – 16) are equipped with benches at the front, back and in a circle in the middle. A recess is left for the transport of bicycles or larger items of luggage. The doors are wide enough for pushchairs and wheelchairs. Mobile hospital beds can even be transported in the cars with 15 seats and 20 standing places. The boarding area is level, so the cable car doesn't have to be held up when bulky items are rolled on or carried.

Car no. 17 has been furnished with a plate of glass, to allow for a direct bird's eye view of the happenings on the riverbank, river and railway line during the journey.

Car no. 18 is called the "urban concept" car. Its bucket seats are reminiscent of the furnishings of a subway car. In the near future, cable car gondolas for public transport might look like this, or somewhat similar. For Doppelmayr, the Koblenz cable car is a point of reference through which to demonstrate how easy, safe and environmentally friendly modern public transport in big cities can be.

Perspectives

Over a very short time, the cable car has become one of Koblenz's main attractions – both for locals and tourists. UNESCO originally approved the operation of a cable car only until the year 2013. Longer use would result in the Middle Rhine Valley being stripped of its status as a *World Cultural Heritage Site*. In the end, however – after many consultations, discussions and even protests – the world heritage committee decided that Koblenz would be allowed to keep the cable car until the year 2026.

This period of use corresponds to the expiration of its technical operational life. At that point, the cable car would have to be dismantled in any case. More and more experts now consider cable cars to be a realistic, economical and environmentally friendly transport option in urban areas.

In their *Human Settlement Programme*, the United Nations reached the conclusion that half the world's population already live in cities. What's more, the structure of settlements is becoming increasingly complex because of the growing distances between home and workplace and the unplanned expansion of cities.

Existing transport infrastructures are already bordering on maximum capacity. Modern cable cars can offer brand new approaches to solving current and future transportation problems. While they used to simply connect two end points, the latest generation of cable cars are already equipped with stations which permit passengers to change between different cable car lines or between cable cars and other forms of public transport.

Short distance transport solutions like this offer a blueprint for the future for cable car operators. Cable cars take only a short time to construct, create a new, unobstructed plane of transport and overcome obstacles with ease. Or, as in Koblenz, they connect the banks of the Rhine with one of the most beautiful viewpoints in the World Cultural Historic Site, the Upper Middle Rhine Valley.

Appendix

Technical Data

Construction/Operation: Doppelmayr Group, Wolfurt, Austria
Design: Werner Sobek Engineering & Design, Stuttgart
Construction Time: 14 months, completed 2010
Cable system: 3S – Tri-cable system (Using two supporting cables and a traction cable)
Weight of the Supporting Cables: 17 tonnes each
Diameter of the Supporting Cables: 54 mm
Diameter of the Traction Cable: 42 mm
Cars: 18 cars for 35 passengers each
car no. 17 with a glass plate, car no. 18 – "urban concept" – with a local public transport design
Weight of Each Car: 3.5 tonnes, including driver mechanism
Cable car length: 890 metres
Free Span between the Supports: 850 metres
Height Difference: 112 metres
Motor: 1300 horsepower; fuel-efficient, electric-powered
Transport Performance per Hour and Direction:
3,000 people/hour at 4.5 m/sec (ca. 16 km/h)
3,800 people/hour at 5.5 m/sec (ca. 20 km/h)
Travel time: 3.3 min at 4.5 m/sec (= 16.2 km/h)